THE VIKINGS

STRUAN REID

Belitha Press

Acknowledgements

Photographic Credits

Cover: Viking Ship Museum, Bygdoy, Norway, fierce human mask from the front of a cart, AD 850
page 1: Arhus Art Museum, Denmark, the Viking god Loki whose lips were sewn together as a punishment, twelfth century
page 3: B.C. Alexander, view of the frozen water and land of Scandanavia
page 4: Mary Evans Picture Library, Britain, a Victorian impression of Vikings invading a foreign land (engraving)
page 6: British Museum, London, whalebone figure of the king from the Lewis chess set, AD 1140
page 8: State Historical Museum, Stockholm, Sweden, silver charm of Thor's Hammer, tenth century
page 10: University Museum of National Antiquities, Oslo, Norway, sword hilt, sixth century
page 12: Werner Forman Archive London/Oslo University, Norway, part of a wooden carving farm the doorway of the church of Hylestad, twelfth century
page 14: University of Trondheim, Norway, whalebone line-winder
page 16: Werner Forman Archive London/University of Oslo, Norway, silver-plated iron brooch, seventh century
page 18: National Museum of Ireland, Dublin, wooden games board, AD 950
page 20: Lund Museum, Sweden, rune stone
page 22: Central Board of National Antiquities, Stockholm, Sweden, Birka necklace, seventh century
page 24: Werner Forman Archive London/Viking Ship Museum, Bygdoy, Norway, Oseberg Ship, AD 850
page 26: Werner Forman Archive London/State Historical Museum, Stockholm, Sweden, Viking helmet from a boat grave, seventh century
page 28: British Museum, London, copper/alloy key

First published in Great Britain in 1993 by
Belitha Press Limited
31 Newington Green, London N16 9PU
Reprinted 1993, 1994

ISBN 1 85561 189 9
Typeset by Amber Graphics, Burgess Hill, West Sussex

British Library Cataloguing in Publication Data CIP data for this book is available from the British Library

Printed in Singapore for Imago

Editor: **Jill A. Laidlaw**
Specialist consultant: **Anne Pearson**, British Museum
Designed by: **John Calvert**
Picture research: **Lesley Coleman**
Illustrated by: **James Field**

CONTENTS

*Words found in **bold** are explained in the glossary on pages 30 and 31*

In Search of the Vikings

In the far North of Europe, in the countries we now call Sweden, Norway and Denmark, lived a fierce race of warriors known as the Vikings. Over a period of about three hundred years from AD790, some of these people left their lands and travelled far and wide. Many sailed across the **Atlantic Ocean** to Iceland, Greenland and North America. Others settled in France, Britain and Russia. Some even travelled as far as Turkey and Iraq.

The Vikings were also merchants and farmers. They wrote wonderful stories called **sagas**. Many of the beautiful things they made can be seen in museums today.

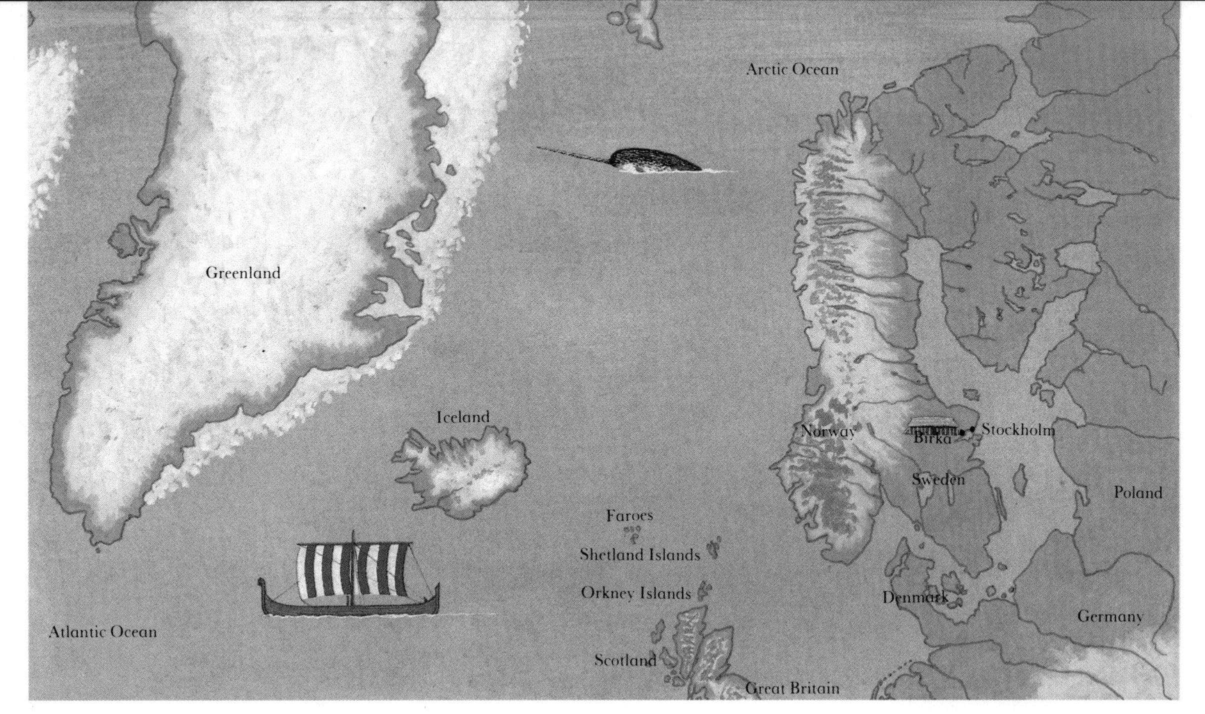

This Victorian engraving (far left) illustrates how later generations of people have imagined the Vikings to be – fierce and bloodthirsty.

This map (above) shows the Viking homelands of Sweden, Norway and Denmark.

If you follow the red line on the globe (left) you can see the incredible distances the Vikings travelled. The circle shows where the Vikings lived.

Your Own Museum

In this book you will see some of the things that the Vikings made and how the Vikings lived during the years of their greatness. By asking questions about these objects we can build up a picture of what it was like to be a Viking. We can look at their sleek longships, their houses and the clothes they wore. We can see some of their strange writing and read about their belief in **Valhalla** and their gods and goddesses.

Q: What is this?
A: This is the king from a Viking chess set. The set was carved from walrus tusks in about AD 1140. The king was the most powerful person in Viking society.

Q: Was there only one king?
A: At the beginning of the Viking age, the land was divided up and ruled over by many kings. As well as kings there were rich landowners called **jarls**. Most people were called **karls** and they usually owned a little land. At the bottom of Viking society were the **thralls**, or slaves.

Q: How did the Vikings govern?
A: The Vikings held open-air meetings called **Things** to discuss important matters and solve problems. Although only men could vote at Things, they often took their families along with them.

This indoor meeting has been called to settle a dispute between two neighbours. The king is listening to all the arguments.

Q: What was this object used for?

A: This small silver charm (5cm long), was worn by a Viking as a protection against evil spirits. It is in the shape of the stone hammer of the Viking god Thor.

Q: Who was Thor?

A: Thor was the god of farming, wind and rain. He had a bright red beard and was very strong. He called his hammer Mjollnir and used it in his battles with giants.

Q: Did the Vikings believe in other gods?

A: The Vikings believed in many gods and goddesses. They all lived in a place called Asgard. **Odin** was the most important of all the Viking gods. The most famous Viking goddess was **Freya**, the goddess of love and death.

Thor strikes terror into the hearts of men and giants. He is brandishing his hammer which flashes with lightning.

DEATH, BURIAL AND VALHALLA

Q: Who did this belong to?
A: This sword hilt was found inside a Viking warrior's grave.

Q: Did Vikings believe in life after death?
A: Viking warriors believed that if they died in battle, their souls would go to a heavenly palace called Valhalla. Here, they would spend most of their time eating and fighting.

A Viking chieftain has died and his body has been laid out in a boat. He is surrounded by a servant and some of his favourite possessions to help him on his journey to Valhalla.

Q: How were they buried?
A: Most Vikings were buried in graves in the ground. When a rich Viking warrior died he was buried in a great wooden chamber. Some very important warriors were even placed in ships and then the ship was buried or burned.

HOME LIFE

Q: Why is this man sucking his thumb?

A: The man has burnt his thumb on the fire. The wooden carving shows him cooking meat over a fire inside his house.

Winter evenings were long and cold. But there were many jobs to do inside the house like weaving, cooking and preparing tools.

Q: What did Viking houses look like?

A: Viking houses are known as longhouses because of their long shape (see illustration on page 19). Inside, there was usually one large room where everyone ate, slept and did the household work.

Q: What was the most important part of the house?

A: The most important area in the house was the fireplace. It was usually in the middle of the room where the family could keep warm, chat and cook food. Smoke from the fire went out through a small hole in the roof.

Q: Was there much furniture in Viking houses?

A: The Vikings kept very little furniture and usually sat on benches. Some had chests to store their belongings in.

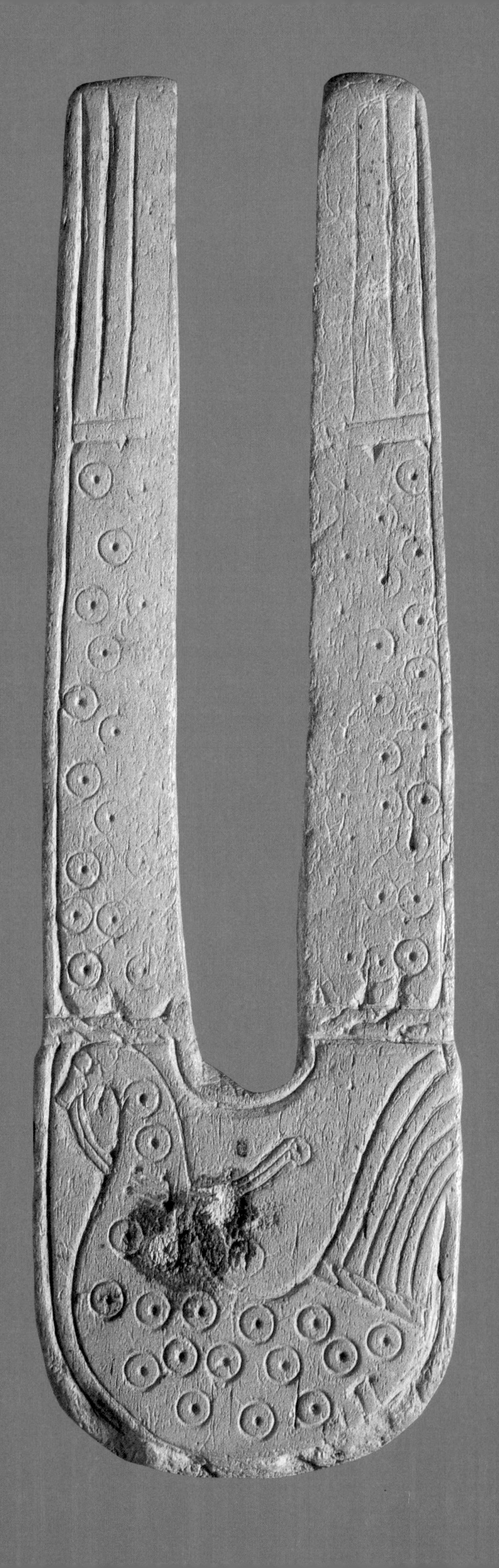

Q: Was this object used for fishing or farming?

A: This was used by a Viking fisherman to wind in his fishing line. It is made of whalebone and is decorated with the outline of a bird.

Q: Did the Vikings do a lot of fishing and hunting?

A: Yes, the Vikings often went out fishing in boats with nets, spears, hooks and lines. They also hunted animals in the forests and birds beside the sea. Large animals like seals, walruses and whales were also hunted.

Q: What other foods did they eat?

A: Most Vikings were farmers and spent much time working in their fields. They grew corn and kept cattle, sheep, goats, pigs and chickens. Beside their houses they grew vegetables like onions and cabbages. They also ate apples, nuts, berries and honey from wild bees when they could find it.

These Vikings are hunting seals with nets and spears. Out at sea, whales are being driven into shallow water where they will be speared by the hunters.

CLOTHES AND APPEARANCE

Q: What would a Viking have used this for?
A: This is a belt buckle. It is made of iron covered with silver and decorated with **precious** stones and **enamel**.

Q: What did the Vikings look like?
A: The Vikings took a lot of care over their appearance. The men often had platted beards and kept their hair long. Both men and women liked to wear all sorts of gold and silver jewellery like brooches, bracelets, rings, armbands and necklaces.

Q: What were their clothes made of?
A: The Vikings made their clothes from wool and **linen** cloth which they wove themselves. The men wore tunics and trousers, while the women wore linen dresses (see illustration). Everybody wore shoes made out of leather. In cold weather they wore thick woollen cloaks.

The Vikings often fastened their clothes at the shoulder with elaborate brooches. Their clothes were sometimes embroidered with beautiful designs. The belt buckle in the photograph is on the belt worn by the Viking man.

18

In their free time, Viking men often organized wrestling matches. The children liked playing ball games, much the same as people today.

Q: Was this board used in a game?

A: Yes, this wooden game board was found in Ireland and was made by Viking craftsmen in AD 950. Two players sat opposite each other and moved pegs across the board rather like the game of draughts.

Q: Did the Vikings play many games?

A: The Vikings liked to play board games during the long, dark winter evenings. They also enjoyed running, horse-racing and wrestling. In winter they went ice-skating on frozen lakes and rivers.

Q: What were their favourite entertainments?

A: Music was one of the things the Vikings liked the most. They played on harps and pipes and children made whistles from the leg bones of birds. Viking men enjoyed telling sagas.

WRITING

The memorial stone is being carved by a craftsman. He is using a wooden **mallet** and an iron **chisel** to cut the runes.

Q: Does this stone show Viking writing?
A: Yes, the stone does have Viking writing carved on it. These letters are called runes. They were invented 2,000 years ago. The runic alphabet had sixteen letters.

Q: Why are they carved on a stone?
A: The Vikings carved on stone instead of writing on paper. The Vikings carved runes on **memorial** stones. The words on this memorial stone say: 'Kaulfr and Autir, they erected this stone in memory of Tumi, their brother, who owned Gusnava.'

Q: Were runes used for other things?
A: The Vikings believed that runes had magical powers. Sometimes runes were carved on metal swords to make them stronger in battle.

TRADE

Q: What has this necklace got to do with trade?
A: This Viking necklace is made of beads of glass, **crystal** and **cornelian**. It is also made up of silver coins from different parts of the world where the Vikings traded.

Q: Did the Vikings travel far to trade?
A: The Vikings did a lot of trade with their close neighbours. But they also traded with people very far away. They carried goods by ship or on horseback over hundreds, sometimes thousands, of kilometres.

Q: What sorts of goods did they exchange?
A: Viking merchants loaded their ships with goods such as honey, wax, furs, glass, cloth and jewellery. In ports as far away as the **Mediterranean**, they would **barter** them for silver coins, wheat, wines, silks and spices.

Foreign merchants have arrived by ship to trade at this Viking market town.

This is a detail of the front of the Oseberg ship. You can see the intricately carved Viking designs.

TRANSPORT AND TRAVEL

Q: Is this a real Viking ship?
A: Yes, it is known as the Oseberg ship. It was found buried in Norway and contained the body of a Viking chieftain. **Archaeologists** were able to **restore** it because it had been **preserved** by the soil it was buried in over a thousand years ago.

Q: How did Vikings travel?
A: Most Vikings lived near the sea. Their main form of transport was by ship. Viking ships were some of the finest ever built.

Q: What is the most famous type of Viking ship?
A: The most famous type of Viking ship is a longship. Longships were made from long planks of wood and were very strong. They were also very slim and sleek and could sail in shallow water as well as on the open sea.

The carved wooden dragonshead on the front of the ship was supposed to frighten the Vikings' enemies.

VIKING WARRIORS

Q: Who wore this?
A: This helmet was once worn by a Viking warrior. It was found in a grave in Sweden and was carefully restored after it was discovered.

Viking warriors have arrived by sea and are attacking a Christian monastery. The monks who escaped later wrote books about the fierceness of the Viking invaders.

Q: Why was it in a grave?
A: Viking warriors believed that after they died they would go and fight battles in Valhalla. So they were often buried with some of their weapons (see page 11).

Q: What weapons did warriors use?
A: Vikings used spears and axes in battle and carried wooden shields covered with leather. Swords were their favourite weapons. They were made of iron and sometimes had handles of gold and silver. Some warriors were so fond of their swords that they gave them nicknames.

VIKING WOMEN

Q: Who looked after this key?

A: Viking women were entrusted with the key to the **storage chest** in a Viking home. Viking women did not have pockets in their clothes. Instead, they carried the things they needed on a long chain.

Q: What did women do?

A: Viking women were responsible for cooking, cleaning, washing and looking after the children. They also spun, wove cloth and made clothes.

Q: Were Viking women important?

A: Women were treated with great respect in Viking society. Some could be very independent, especially if they were rich. Women were allowed to choose their own husbands or stay single if they wished. They could own land and houses and work as farmers and merchants. When their husbands were away, women were in charge of the household and had to defend it if it was attacked.

This Viking woman owns her house and farm. She is instructing her farm helpers who are ploughing a field for corn. You can see her keys on a chain attached to her clothes.

GLOSSARY

archaeologist: someone who discovers things about the past by finding and examining what remains of the past.

Atlantic Ocean: the ocean that separates Europe and Africa from America.

barter: to barter is to exchange one object for another of equal value.

chisel: a tool that is used for cutting into things such as wood and stone. One end of a chisel is a handle. Fixed into the handle is a shaft of metal sharpened into a triangular-shaped point.

cornelian: a beautiful mineral, usually red in colour.

crystal: a clear, hard rock that looks a bit like ice. Crystal comes in many different colours.

enamel: a glassy coating that can be brushed on to metal and many other surfaces. Enamel comes in many different colours and is used to decorate or protect something.

Freya: the Viking goddess of love and death. The Vikings believed that Freya could start wars on Earth.

jarls: were the richest people in Viking society. Jarls owned a great deal of land and commanded the Viking armies and navy.

karls: most Vikings were karls. Karls owned a small piece of land which they farmed. Karls made up the bulk of the Viking army and navy.

linen: a lightweight material made from a plant called flax, usually white in colour.

mallet: a hammer that has a large head, usually made out of wood.

Mediterranean: the land near the Mediterranean Sea, which is the sea that separates southern Europe, Africa and the Middle East.

memorial: a piece of writing that is written in order to remember the dead. A memorial can say many things such as how long someone lived for, where they lived or what they did during their life.
Odin: the most important of all Viking gods. Odin reigns from the palace of **Valhalla** where he welcomes the souls of dead warriors. Odin is married to **Freya** and their son is Thor (see pages 8-9).
precious: something that is very valuable and rare.
preserved: when something has been preserved it has been prevented from rotting. Sometimes this is because of certain chemicals that have been added to the object or food. Salt is used to preserve many things. Objects can also be preserved if they are protected from harmful air or moisture.
restore: to restore something is to put it back into working order, to make it as beautiful or as solid as it was before it decayed.
sagas: the sagas are long, very detailed Viking stories and legends.
storage chest: a large box with a lock and key that is used to store valuable things.
Thing: the name given to the Viking parliament. This parliament was an open-air meeting where all free men voted. There were different types of Things, ones that could involve an entire village or the whole country.
thralls: slaves who worked the land. Thralls were often born into slavery or were prisoners from wars.
Valhalla: the heavenly palace where Viking heroes and warriors believed they went after death.

INDEX

A number in **bold** shows that the entry is illustrated on that page.
Words in **bold** can be found in the glossary on pages 30–31.